P9-AQO-200

CREATING
BEAUTY
INTERIORS

CREATING BEAUTY

INTERIORS

KATHRYN SCOTT

PRINCIPAL PHOTOGRAPHY BY WILLIAM ABRANOWICZ

WRITTEN WITH JUDITH NASITIR

RIZZOLI
NEW YORK

New York Paris London Milan

FOR MY FAMILY—PAST AND PRESENT—
WHO ARE MY VERY ESSENCE.

CONTENTS

INTRODUCTION

I have always been quite serious in my attempts to create beauty and transform the world around me, even when that wasn't my professional intent. It took me quite a while to realize that there were actually careers that centered on such pursuits. I studied to be a painter and later made a concerted effort to become an artist. I became an interior designer almost by chance. For years, I switched my focus between interior design and art. But whether I was an aspiring painter in front of an easel or practicing interior design, instinct and intuition have always propelled me forward in the desire to transform my surroundings.

I approach interior design as I do painting. I don't try to force anything. Instead, I let things unfold in their own time, once the place tells me what it wants to be and my concept for it becomes clear. Building on that vision, I continually reassess the overall composition as it develops to make sure all components—light and dark, curved and straight, hard and soft, transparent and solid, and so on—are in balance. This requires a constant critical eye and a willingness to adjust as I go. I wait for a visual moment to occur that pulls me in an unexpected direction and leads me to an invented solution. I look for that spark of the special, that one detail that will point the way to the exceptional. What matters most to me is to find a solution that is unanticipated, unpredictable, unique. If I can't find what I am looking for, my instinct is to make it myself. When I can't, I hunt for an artisan with the requisite skills.

The hands-on approach appears to be inherited from the women in my family. My mother was always busy crafting tabletops from mosaics or other items for her rooms. In her last home—a modest 1950s beach house in Florida inherited from her father—she hired an architect to upgrade the original bathrooms and the kitchen. When he advised her to tear the house down and start over, she did just that. By herself. In one of life's strange twists, I happened to be grappling with the first phase of renovating our old Brooklyn townhouse, learning how to get my own hands dirty at the same time.

Early on, I discovered that something beautiful can become even more so as it reveals its age and experience. The same holds true for the rooms in which we live. Certainly, every aspect of a home—materials, furnishings, art, and accessories—should be authentic, personal, and intrinsically functional for the present lifestyle of the people who dwell in it. But why not appreciate the various patinas that develop in spaces with history, rather than compulsively scrub them away? As the Japanese concept of wabi-sabi celebrates, the life of the object represents the wisdom gained in that lifetime. When our homes include connections to our past and our present, as well as some glimmer of our future, they feel alive.

My first inkling of the importance of time as an intrinsic aspect of beauty emerged, not surprisingly, on my first trip to Europe. I remember visiting Versailles, which hadn't yet been buffed and polished back to its current state of gilded perfection. The interiors then were almost falling apart.

OPPOSITE: A renovation of our Brooklyn brownstone brought harmony and cohesiveness to the rear facade.

The joints in the boiserie were exposed, making it possible to see how the walls of the room were constructed. I remember thinking at the time how pure that paneling was as an expression of human art, invention, and intention.

I trace my affinity for antiques to my father's mother. Her home was quite modest, but full of Americana antiques that she used day to day, from her prized Windsor chairs down to the nickel silver spoons with which she set the table. You entered a different era in her house. That fascinated me, as did the fact that she had collected many of her furnishings during the Depression. In those Dust Bowl days, she and her niece-in-law would periodically go antiquing. The two of them would drive a truck from Texas to the East Coast, proceeding from door to door, asking about unwanted old things, and filling up the back of the truck with their purchases. Once home, the two of them would fix those broken-down pieces and trade them back and forth. My grandmother's garage in those years must have been jammed with newly salvaged furnishings waiting for her attention. Over time, she furnished the entire house with her repaired, refinished, and repurposed pieces, authentic relics of American history. When I visited, she would let me stay up late (then a privilege for adults only), telling me the stories of where she had found each of her antiques. By the time I was eight, she was advising me on the value of buying Windsor chairs, should I ever find them. In retrospect, that seems like such a funny thing to say to an eight-year-old. Yet it resonated.

When I was in my mid-twenties and able to start purchasing my own furniture, Windsor chairs were among the first things I acquired. Eventually, I had an entire collection of them, each one different, around my dining table. Realizing that the association of those chairs with my grandmother tied me directly to my childhood, I began to feel that my surroundings represented an aspect of my personal history—the people who were so dear to me were still present through the objects and furnishings that we had discussed or shared. Perhaps that is the reason I am attracted to unique patinas, the evidence of age, to antiques and architectural salvage, and to older things that have life in them and show the lives they've already led.

I also trace my preference for earthy simplicity to my mother. My parents had a contemporary home. Many of its components had been made to measure, which was surprising in a builder's house. Yet the builder was an architect, and because he had designed the house for his own family, the interiors were anything but generic. The rooms incorporated a number of smart innovations; in my room, there were a customized, child-sized desk and custom cabinets. These individualized aspects of the house awakened me to the idea that one could create a home—and everything in it—to suit a particular person and purpose. The experience of growing up in those rooms encouraged my belief that I could be the one who conceived, created, and directed what was made.

I had become quite interested in interior design my senior year at Southern Methodist University, though I didn't think of it then as a possible profession. (The one course available covered basic spatial analysis and drafting.) As a student, I'd transformed the surfaces of my successive apartments with decorative ideas inspired by my travels thus far: stapling sheets to walls for an upholstered appearance, painting Persian tiles by hand on blank bathroom walls, applying trompe l'oeil architectural

OPPOSITE: A scholar's stone from Lake Tai in China is one of the many objects at our country house that bears deep personal meaning.

details to a vestibule ceiling to suggest a groin vault. As a senior, I decided to do a more comprehensive interior renovation. Instinct told me that endless possibilities existed for making that space unique: introducing clean lines, curved doors, and other architectural features, features that were aspects of my developing sensibility. What I learned was that creating transformation hands-on involved far more effort than expected.

Completely up in the air about what to do career-wise after graduation with my double major in Italian and Studio Art, I found myself one day flipping through *Interior Design* magazine. An ad for an apprenticeship in New York with Hans Krieks, a well-regarded designer of office furniture and interiors, caught my eye. What appealed most was the hands-on nature of the training. Mr. Krieks accepted only twelve students a year, and I became one of them. After my first month in the program, Mr. Krieks died unexpectedly. Instead of returning to Texas, I stayed put.

What next? A friend of my father's introduced me to Lella and Massimo Vignelli. At the interview, I showed Lella photographs of the apartment I'd renovated in Dallas, and the abstract black-and-white images seemed to appeal to her. She asked if I could make models, draw, and so on. Then she suggested that if she chose to hire me, I should intern at the firm for free for six months since I lacked any formal design training. That seemed like a great bargain to me: school without tuition. I headed home to draw furniture and make little models, which I dropped off at the reception desk a week later. (I had no idea what I was doing!) Two weeks later, Lella called. And that was that.

After almost three years of being immersed in design with the Vignellis, I wanted to try to become the artist I aspired to be. I enrolled at the Art Students League of New York and the National Academy of Design, though

I kept my hand in the interior design world with several small projects. In retrospect, I realize just how formative my time with the Vignellis was, how unique their point of view was, and how their influence still percolates in me. The way they used simple materials to maximum effect is the essence of what I do.

During those years of painting and freelancing, I purchased a duplex apartment in a historic, nineteenth-century Italianate brownstone in Brooklyn Heights and began renovating it. That proved to be a major turning point in my design education. Coming on-site periodically to check on the progress of the job engaged me so much, I began to come back every day. Eventually, I became part of the construction team, applying myself to every task imaginable. Each day offered new lessons in the implications of every design decision: why things might take longer than expected, why they might become more expensive than hoped, why some things went wrong because they were a lot more difficult than thought, and what options existed to resolve questions not answered in the drawings and plans. I began to understand fully how much work—and expertise—went into making manifest what I had imagined. I learned to appreciate the complications and the possibilities: when the right solution does not exist ready-made, the imagination can create one.

In the midst of the renovation, I remember having dinner with some friends, one of whom was studying to be an interior designer. She asked if I would like to see her homework. Looking at her drawings and sketches, it dawned on me that through my passion for creating the spaces that I wished to inhabit, I had taught myself to understand design by doing it.

Much of my design education over the years has also come through observation, such as visiting house museums; studying how earlier builders, architects, and designers had resolved similar issues to those that came up in my Brooklyn brownstone; investigating how they drew their plans; and discovering how they accomplished their goals faster. My curiosity about the beauty of the built environment struck me on my first trip to Europe, when I was a teenager. That summer, my father was working overseas and had taken an apartment for the family in France. It was such an introduction to luxury. We rented a car, so I was able to drive here and there. We spent a week in Venice, Florence, and Milan, staying in fabulously beautiful rooms in wonderfully grand hotels, and eating in all the best restaurants. On side trips to Burgundy and Lyon, we did the same. The old buildings, the light filtering onto the narrow streets, the architectural details, various senses of proportion and scale, and age that was respected rather than torn down—experiencing these places immersed me in a totally different visual world than the one I had grown up with and knew so well. That education continues to this day. And as I continue to travel and my tastes change, there is always more to learn, explore, and absorb.

After a decade of working alone, I put painting aside and refocused on interior design, a much more collaborative undertaking. One day, in the ad pages of the *New York Times*, I happened into a once-in-a-lifetime opportunity: a Russian businessman was assembling a team of professionals to design and build various ventures around the former Soviet Union, including the interiors for the dacha (a log-cabin summerhouse) of the President of Tatarstan. On day three of the job, off I flew. Given the scarcity of supplies after the Iron Curtain came down, the businessman opted to send ahead what we thought would be the necessary machinery and materials, as well as a crew of carpenters.

Which meant that when something wouldn't work, we had to fix it ourselves or find someone who could. If neither of those options were possible, we had to change the design according to what we could find locally. That combination of flexibility, economy, and invention continues to drive me today. Mine is not an aesthetic of too much, nor one that tolerates waste. I always try to repurpose anything useful, whatever it may be.

Shortly after returning from Russia, I started to focus on my own business. When a team member from the Russian project recommended me to her parents—their house in Scarsdale, New York, needed an update—that prodded me into following my own vision instead of trying to figure out someone else's. With them as my first clients—they remain clients today—I began developing my own design business in earnest. Gradually, my office grew.

When foreign business in China started to flourish, my husband, the artist Wenda Gu, suggested I try to establish a satellite design studio there. On our first trip to China together in 1999, I could not help but notice that Shanghai, his hometown, had a treasure trove of beautiful old buildings, all of them falling apart. I was captivated. Although I knew neither the language nor the local customs, business or otherwise, I found myself inspired to try to restore and rejuvenate one or more of those structures to work with the modern lifestyle. At the time, the Shanghainese were razing their historic houses at an alarming rate and throwing up the modern high-rises that they felt would be their giant leap forward into the twenty-first century. I desperately wanted to show them how beautiful the old houses could be and, in so doing, possibly change attitudes about tearing them down. My husband's brother introduced us to an opportunity to buy a repossessed house, a grand red-and-gray-brick 1906

Colonial in the center of Shanghai. With his help, we were able to acquire the property, which we intended to upgrade for a commercial rental.

The house was completely dilapidated, with a potential for transformation that only people involved in design and art would see. The structure needed a major overhaul—new roof, windows, everything. White ceramic tile covered large portions of the red-and-gray-brick exterior. At that time, it was still possible to find people in China to fabricate all kinds of custom work relatively inexpensively. The opportunity to customize everything was so exciting, and I chose to use materials and commission architectural elements that I could never afford in the States. The house had an outdoor veranda, which I enclosed with custom-made glass doors in delicate bronze frames. The gates and balcony railings had ornamental flowers carved and cast in bronze. Everything was handmade. It took a year to unearth a metalworker who could deliver precisely what I designed. Our eventual tenant—a restaurant and wine bar—hired me to do the interiors. That design was published internationally and received many compliments from the local government. Unfortunately, it didn't inspire the immediate wave of restoration—or grow my office there—in the way that I had hoped. After five years, our tenants outgrew the space. The house has remained the same, and today it is a very fancy kindergarten.

Trying to run an office in a country where one neither knows the customs nor speaks the language is an exciting venture and an ambitious one, but it is also beyond difficult, even when family and friends can help. My husband spent far more time and effort attempting to assist me with my office than he had anticipated when

he suggested the idea. Because the additional Chinese projects I had hoped for never quite materialized—despite all the inquiries and requests for proposals—I ultimately shuttered the office. My husband uses the space as his studio when he's in Shanghai.

Each generation finds its own future, even as it carries the past forward. Perhaps that's why I find it enormously comforting to live with things that mattered so much to me growing up. Certainly every time I look at or touch the pieces that my parents, grandparents, and prior generations cared for, I am reminded of them. Some of us may not have any traces of family history; others may have many. It's not always possible to use every last piece, but if there is any way to incorporate a portion of these items, that is my first choice.

Every project comes with a set of criteria: the desires of the people who will dwell in it, the demands of the architecture of the room itself, the functional necessities that must be respected, and an entire series of aesthetic considerations that make the challenges of design interesting. Ultimately, the designer's role is to ensure that each room will look—and be—its best. So the designer must make sure that in each unique, created space, function is an element of beauty. The idea, however, that a living space should look like this year's trend seems out of tune, perhaps even devoid of personal meaning. Maybe a portion of it should incorporate what's fashionable now, but not all of it. Life doesn't start today; there is history behind us. Our interiors will transform over the years as we do. In that way, they resemble us, not just our tastes at a particular time. Like us, our homes are never finished. There is always the question of what comes next.

OPPOSITE: An antique Philadelphia Windsor chair is right at home in our daughter's Brooklyn bedroom.

THE LIFE OF A HOUSE

Houses live multiple lives. Like people, they evolve over time. This is especially true of historic houses, like our five-story, nineteenth-century Italianate brownstone in Brooklyn Heights. One of three sister structures, it belonged for many years to the Church of St. Ann and the Holy Trinity. By 1986, when my story with it begins, developers were converting it from a single-family dwelling into a co-op building with two duplex residences (garden and parlor floors; third and fourth floors) and a floor-through apartment at the top.

Although the entire house now belongs to us, it hasn't always. Each phase of acquisition has occasioned significant renovations that have played a formative role in my career as an interior designer and in my ongoing design education. My first toehold here was the middle duplex, purchased just as the developer's contractors were about to install the finishing touches. At the time I was fixated on being an artist, but I had enough practical design experience to know that I wanted to create something personal, to follow my own vision. Stopping the contractors before they installed their off-the-shelf cabinets, moldings, and hardware gave me the freedom to transform the apartment without having to start entirely from scratch.

Historic houses always offer up architectural clues that lead you into certain design decisions. I knew I wanted our duplex to feel fluid and

OPPOSITE: Donated by the Brooklyn Historical Society, the vintage radiator in our entry hall enhances the period feeling. The entry walls take on a fresco-like quality after being stripped and refinished with a wash over surviving patches of wallpaper glue. PAGE 16: A remnant of an earlier decoration, too beautiful to remove, reemerged during the process. PAGE 17: We relocated the original pier mirror to the end of hall to add reflected light. One of the works from my husband's *Forest of Stone Steles* series hangs prominently. PAGES 18–19: In our living room, my own designs in porcelain, sterling and glass, and wood cohabit with Wenda's work in ink and his video chair. A fragment of a marble statue introduces the ancient into the mix.

993 2001 in Xian, China. 碑林－唐詩後著之

稿於辛巳年谷文達著並製碑於西安

cohesive. I also thought the aesthetic should be classic enough to be believable, without re-creating a historically accurate Victorian interior. As I began looking for design direction, I found myself influenced by Americana, Art Deco, and a combination of eighteenth-century French and Swedish Gustavian architecture. From these references came a number of defining elements, including the French doors, wainscoting, and wide-plank floors.

A chance visit to Newport, Rhode Island, before we started the renovations had an unexpected impact on my thinking. All the beautifully handcrafted details in The Breakers and the other grand mansions influenced me deeply—there were engraved brass switch plates and unique hardware, classic proportions and hidden doors, bronze railings and beautiful patinas. Nothing was standard. Each element was individual and unique to each house, shaped and proportioned just so. Once we had hired a contractor, we went back to Newport with permission to investigate those wonderfully specific, old-school details, such as those found in the installation of the hidden doors.

As the renovation got underway, I would visit the space regularly to check on progress. I enjoyed being at the construction site, and there were often questions to answer when I came. The template for the stair rail was my first hands-on project here. I had done a small sketch to show the contractor and workmen my idea for the design, but it was impossible to scale it up and get the form and proportions exactly right. Sharpie in

PAGE 20: A reproduction of an old Chinese tieback brings in a touch of Shanghai, my husband's hometown. PAGE 21: The stone mantel was relocated from the original dining room downstairs. To make the fireplace appear larger, an Italian stucco surround embraces it from floor to ceiling. OPPOSITE: Ming dynasty stools pull up to our marble coffee table, which was hand-carved in Wenda's Xi'an stone studio. My mother's pianoforte nests against one wall.

hand, I drew what the design should be, life-size, on some cardboard the workmen had set up. The experience was transformative. Every day from then on, I began working as part of the crew, offering help with any task that presented itself: preparing surfaces for the tile man, helping the carpenter, nailing the pegs into the wide-plank flooring, sanding moldings, making calls for the contractor—whatever needed doing.

Enough traces of the original moldings remained that I was able to copy or adapt the different profiles and add them where they hadn't survived—and where they made sense—to create a visually coherent history. With the surroundings taking shape, I began searching for other components for these rooms that felt equally authentic and true. No one then was re-creating period bath fittings or fixtures, so I began to search for architectural salvage. At Urban Archaeology, I found them: an antique tub, sink, rainfall showerhead, radiator knobs with labels, lighting, a heated towel bar, and more, all with the cracks and the crazing that I love, which give the surfaces much more dimension. Lenny Schechter, one of the founders of Urban Archaeology, made it work; when the necessary parts were missing, he had them fabricated. I also hunted for antique hardware of all kinds. Suddenly, I had become like my grandmother, with a bucket of old doorknobs in the utility basement.

Our second major chapter with the house began around 2001, when my mother wanted to be closer to us. Coincidentally, our downstairs

OPPOSITE: The other side of the living room connects to the dining room and kitchen via an arched passage added to correct problematic proportions and also house the powder room. The ceiling moldings replicate a surviving original detail. Atop my grandparents' Chippendale secretary are pots from different eras and cultures. Silk velvet pillows on the linen-slipcovered settee and a Steuben table made from roots attest to my love of combining the rustic with the refined.

neighbors were moving to London. They agreed to sell their garden-level duplex, which we then completely revamped for my mother to make the spaces on both levels more graceful. Many of the details of this renovation also hearkened back to those we saw on that trip to Newport years before. Instead of moving the kitchen off the parlor floor, where the developers had placed it in this duplex, I combined it with the existing dining room and recast the joined spaces as a repurposed library lined with glassed-in cabinets and floor-to-ceiling shelves. Our dining table was my mother's; she had it made for a house that she lived in years ago. Her china fills our cabinets, along with some pieces from one of my grandmothers. In our living room are some of my other grandmother's pieces and my mother's piano.

When our longtime neighbors in the floor-through at the top of the house decided they were ready to move, we purchased that apartment. That's when we tackled the back of the house and the outside spaces as well. We changed mismatched windows, doors, and iron gates to give the facade a unified appearance and added the staircase down to the garden.

We have never restored the house to its single-family floor plan, although I know it would be more elegant to do so. It would also require tearing out much of the existing work, and that is not my way.

OPPOSITE: Custom glass-fronted cabinets and a rolling ladder suggest that the dining room was once a library. Bronze-legged chairs of my design pull up to my mother's table. PAGES 28–29: Family china fills the shelves. PAGE 30: A period bowl and an original mantel share a decorative kinship. PAGE 31: Original plaster details read as texture against the architectural simplicity of the iron chandelier. PAGE 32: The cooking island's slate front can double as a blackboard. PAGE 33: The kitchen's fittings are contemporary, but placed in an old-world way. PAGES 34–35: Windsor and Queen Anne chairs circle the wood-and-bronze table I created for my office.

OPPOSITE: To give the second-floor kitchen a historical look, I painted the stove hood. The Chinese stove from my husband's childhood sits on the counter. Made on-site, tiger maple cabinets feel like a period luxury. PAGE 38: Tiled in Venetian glass, this wall adds a subtle shimmer. PAGE 39: The antique porcelain faucet has a re-machined interior. Caramel onyx inlaid into the maple counter protects the area around the sink. PAGES 40–41: In our bedroom, a Hudson Valley kas stores office samples and client information. One of Wenda's hair panels, part of his larger *United Nations* series, hangs over the fireplace. The Santa Fe side table and wing chair are family pieces. The Albert Cheuret sconce is a replica. PAGE 42: The master bedroom overlooks the garden. PAGE 43: Beside our bed, a Ming dynasty–inspired side table supports a battery-operated twig-based lamp of my design.

PAGE 44: I designed a decorative drain for the bathroom floor as a unique solution to alleviate shower spillage. PAGE 45: Vintage fittings and fixtures in the master bath helped create an illusion of the house's early life. OPPOSITE: Painted with encaustic, plaster moldings mimic the texture of the terra-cotta gargoyle. PAGES 48–49: In the master bedroom, a Chinese pigskin-covered painted box tops a stack of Americana chests. A visit to The Breakers in Newport, Rhode Island, inspired these hidden doors with made-for-the-occasion keyhole pulls. PAGES 50–51: A horsehair mattress finishes the reproduction Ming dynasty opium bed. When our daughter was small, she used the antique child's chair to do her Chinese homework.

MATERIALS OF EXPRESSION

Wood, stone, metal, glass, lime plaster, lime paint: these and other materials are the media that designers use to bring the world of interiors into being, our three-dimensional paints and canvas. Each has an essential self: hard, soft, luminous, opaque, delicate, rigid, feminine, masculine, and so on. Each takes on a different personality depending on the way it is treated (molded, cast, pressed, cut, turned, or carved) and finished (polished, painted, or sandblasted, to name a few). And each has its own color spectrum, which contributes to its overall presence. So it seems almost an understatement to say that a home becomes what it is through its unique palette of materials and the way each finds expression in the various rooms.

Because design is about relationships, I am always thinking about contrast and context when I choose a palette of materials for each project. There is a particular kind of beauty that occurs, for example, when a thin metal with a dull sheen sits next to the earthiness of a wooden slab highlighted by the transparency of glass. Or when a piece of antique brass has sections with verdigris alongside parts that are polished. Even the subtlest differences in appearance can contribute to a great effect. Continuing accents of one material or those of a similar kind—blackened steel and bronze are two favorites—can tie together a room. They can also unify the various spaces under one roof. In a kitchen, for example, a motif like blackened-steel banding may outline all the appliances and woodwork in a way that brings the different elements into balance. In that same house, an exterior iron railing may meet a bronze front door that opens into a foyer with a bronze-railed interior stair and

hardware of especially fine quality. Such touches are all of a kind, a family in their way.

Every material comes with a set of expectations about how, where, and in what form to use it. I like to upend those whenever possible, but always with good reason. For the renovation of a historic home in Brooklyn, for example, I decided to line the interior of a closet with curly maple lumber. This is not done much anymore, as today we mostly put highly figured woods where we can see them. For technical reasons, we also usually opt for veneers rather than lumber. But this house dated to the turn of the twentieth century. Because I was trying to reproduce a feeling of how people in those days had thought about and worked with materials, the choice to go with lumber instead of veneer seemed very appropriate.

I love that during fabrication and finishing, the surfaces of certain materials can take on gradations of color and sheen in ways that are beyond our control. It is impossible to predict accurately, for example, how sheets of rolled steel for a custom stove hood will look after they are heated, joined, and patinated. The material simply does what it wants each time, regardless. The result is always uniquely beautiful, with its own spectrum of hues, textures, and shine. Some areas will absorb the light. Others will reflect it. I could not create a painting more stunning than a piece of that steel. And I couldn't duplicate it, either. It is art in itself.

Real luxury is living with the beauty of these materials. They don't have to be fancy. What matters is that their essence comes through clearly enough so that we can see their truth, honest and sublime.

PARIS MATCH

There's a kind of luxury that has nothing to do with show and everything to do with discovery. That is the story of this four-bedroom house in Brooklyn, which has spare, elegant rooms filled with subtle design surprises.

After living in Paris for years, this family of five moved back across the Atlantic to be closer to their relatives. They wanted a home that would feel at least a bit like the city they had left behind. So we reinvented, demolishing an existing residence down to one wall and completely rebuilding the exterior and interior architecture around it before embarking on the interior design. French architect Claude Puaux collaborated on the new front facade of limestone, with its look of Le Marais; we built it with stone he had custom cut in a yard outside Paris.

Since we were essentially starting from scratch, we were able to establish proportions and use materials (like plaster, stone, and iron) associated with the style of older houses they loved. They preferred their rooms to be minimal, though rich in texture. And they brought no furniture with them. Thus, each piece of furniture, artwork, lighting, and all the artisan details—custom iron railings, metal trim around kitchen cabinets, an acid-etched steel stove hood, and others—gained an extra resonance.

The front door opened to a double-height living room, a serene, stone-floored space where simplicity reigned in shades of warm and cool white. Toward the rear of that same room was the dining room, organized around a live-edge wooden slab table. Custom benches, precisely matched to the table's varying widths, provided an unexpected seating alternative.

PAGE 52: Every material has a distinctive character and personality that different finishes can enhance and even transform. Heating and patination, for example, transform rolled steel for a one-of-a-kind stove hood into a uniquely beautiful surface of color, texture, and shine. OPPOSITE: In the double-height living room, dark woods and metals bring a subtle, neutral palette of warm and cool shades into high focus. The Christian Liaigre lamp and sofa set off a painting by Tom Brydelsky.

In the kitchen, we opted for frosted glass fronts inset into the custom cabinets to reveal the shadowy presence of the dishes and other necessities. An adjacent breakfast area centered on a cement-top table with a bronze base cast to look like wood, down to the grain. Pulled up to that table were classic Saarinen chairs with leather seat cushions and backs of hand-painted canvas.

One level down was the den. We left a portion of that space open to the breakfast room above, which acted as a skylight. For TV watching, the seating group faced the wall so that at the press of a button, blackout shades, a projector, and a screen would all descend from above. Storage walls in cerused oak gave gravity to the opposite corner.

One flight up, the entire floor was given over to the master suite. The bedroom, entered via a pocket door based on historical French styles, nested at the back of the house; the bath luxuriated at the front. In the middle was a dressing room outfitted with closets on all four walls.

The top of the house had three bedrooms and two baths, both with skylights. At the rear, the largest bedroom, en suite with its bath (tub and shower separate, like a luxury hotel), featured a cabinet hidden in the wall for the TV and dresser drawers; two steel armoires with a heavy patina of rust were added for storage and a computer desk. The two bedrooms at the front shared a bath, which separated the sink area from the shower via a frosted-glass door, so two people can use the space without impinging on each other's privacy.

OPPOSITE: A silk rug adds a quiet, reflective texture underfoot. Anchoring the seating area is a bespoke coffee table of Thassos marble on an iron base. The pendant fixture is by David Weeks. PAGES 58–59: Stained cerused-oak cabinets set off the family's collection of scrimshaw and bone-inlaid boxes. PAGE 60: A live-edge dining table provides an organic contrast. PAGE 61: We had benches made to mirror the curve of the table's edge. PAGES 62–63: A frosted mirror wall above the Calacatta marble backsplash adds a luminous glow to the kitchen. PAGE 64: A faux chest of drawers opens into surprise stairs for access to the roof terrace. PAGE 65: The breakfast room overlooks the family room below.

OPPOSITE: The juxtaposition of classical and contemporary French styles repeats throughout the house. The detailing in Victor Carollo's bespoke metalwork even reproduces the variations of patina that come with wear. PAGE 68: Iron casement-window hardware adds a decorative detail to simple china cabinets. PAGE 69: Minimalist pilasters flanking the china cabinet conceal additional storage. Technical difficulties with upholstering led us to paint a damask-inspired pattern directly onto the chairbacks. PAGE 70: The linear pattern in my Gallery desk repeats in the chair's leather strapping. PAGE 71: A French steel bed is a happy reminder of years spent living in Paris. PAGES 72–73: The pale silhouette of the custom iron railings looks like a shadow through the French doors. PAGE 74: A Cor-Ten steel cabinet hides a computer desk while providing a striking artistic patina. PAGE 75: In a guest bedroom, a stack of antique luggage serves as a night table.

FITTING ROOMS

Many of us think that the bigger the living space, the better. But a small residence with carefully selected furnishings and fine details can be just as beautiful as a large one, especially when every last square inch of space is given serious thought and put to work in a graceful way. That was the premise behind the design of this one-bedroom apartment on Manhattan's Upper West Side.

The floor plan was somewhat odd, with a long hall that connected the living room, dining room, and kitchen area to the bedroom. The client liked the idea of this pathway because it made the apartment feel more expansive. To give it additional purpose, we transformed it into a gallery-like expanse with a new floor, a shallow soffit for lighting, and a metal display shelf.

The client wanted his living room to be comfortable and serene, and to reflect his personal interests. A photo of Antarctica that he took provided the starting point. We enlarged the image, hung it as a focal point, and used it as inspiration for the rest of the room's elements, from the rock-shaped, fiberglass coffee table to the shimmery palette of blues and icy tones. He specifically asked for a bar, which we fit into a tall cabinet. For dining, we found a vintage table that collapses down to a compact surface but opens up to seat ten. (Drum side tables pull up to the table as stools for guests when necessary.)

For the client's home office, we created a customized work space—a cabinet-like construction with a desk, drawers, pullout surfaces, and

OPPOSITE: A shelf and proper lighting transform this long hallway into a gallery space for a rotating display of the owner's collected artworks, including Wenda's folding scroll.
PAGES 78–79: From the pillow fabric to the overall color palette, I conceived the living room concept around an enlarged and mounted photograph of Antarctica taken by the owner.
PAGE 80: The coffee table resembles a large river stone—an essential, if simple, form.
PAGE 81: With a modified interior, an old Chinese cabinet converted beautifully into a bar; a tree stump found in our woods provides a focal point on high.

storage space. Because he is an audiophile, we paid very close attention to his home-entertainment unit; custom built with a textured veneer of unusual thickness and unexpected coloration, it accommodates all of his equipment, organized and placed just so.

The kitchen was so compact that every decision emphasized workability and efficiency. A cutout in the counter opposite the oven made it possible for him to back far enough away from the oven to peer straight inside it when its door was open. Easy to wipe down, a glass backsplash and high-gloss lacquered cabinetry helped create the illusion of depth and tonal variation through their reflective qualities.

In the bedroom, as elsewhere, we hid as much storage as possible so that the space would feel open. To establish unified views, the objects on the open shelving were carefully curated for color. To conceal storage drawers built into the base of the bed, we devised a tailored slipcover with corner zippers. For pure sensual pleasure, textures ranged from plush to smooth.

The bath was tiny, so it required the most streamlined kind of space planning. A sliding door minimized the shower's footprint. Encasing the vanity in a wooden column created an opportunity for additional storage via hidden drawers; concealing the medicine cabinet's three compartments with individual mirrors did the same.

Working on this interior reminded me just how powerful design can be: when a home is small, every last detail can make a big, beautiful difference.

OPPOSITE: Perfect for small apartments, this dining table folds down to console size and opens up to seat nine; the stool can double as extra seating. The Ipnos light from Flos is a personal favorite, because it lights up an entire room, even with its minimalist structure. PAGE 84: In the client's home office in the living room, cabinetry hides all sorts of paperwork; storage under the radiator cover holds desk supplies. PAGE 85: As an audiophile, the client had very specific requirements for his audio equipment. The dark grass-cloth lining the A/V cabinet visually unifies the system's components.

OPPOSITE: In the tiny galley kitchen, glossy lacquered cabinetry—an unusual choice for me—and a glass backsplash brightened the kitchen with myriad reflected colors. Cutting away the counter's corner allowed room for opening the oven door and looking directly inside. PAGES 88–89: An easy-to-clean glass backsplash introduces a touch of luminosity. PAGES 90–91: Mohair and linen feel very luxurious together and masculine enough for a man's bedroom. PAGE 92: Miscellaneous objects add restrained visual drama to the bedroom. PAGE 93: Because these two shelving units are the apartment's only options for displaying collections, it was important to curate the grouping carefully for color, silhouette, and shape.

UP ON THE ROOF

The challenge of trying to create a home out of very unusual spaces has always felt to me rather like catnip must to a cat: irresistible. This duplex, three-bedroom penthouse, which nestles under the mansard roof of a landmarked Beaux Arts building on Central Park West, had that kind of appeal. Not only did the sloped roof make for rooms with interesting volumes, but the dwelling also had its own tower topped by a cupola. So how could I resist when David Foley, of Foley Fiore Architecture in Cambridge, Massachusetts, invited me to work on the interiors? He and I had collaborated before, so I knew we shared a similar approach and aesthetic.

When the homeowners decided to move to this apartment, they made it clear that they wanted a contemporary look, neutral and open. This was a complete departure from the style of the home they were leaving behind, a very traditional, antiques-filled residence on the other side of Central Park. Only a few favorite pieces came with them across town. We chose—or designed—the balance of the furnishings (and everything else) just for the residence.

The first step of the transformation involved stripping away the existing walls to expose the roof's structure and supporting truss system. Those architectural elements had such strong character (and such a distinctive industrial beauty) that they started to become the theme of the design. The second broad stroke opened up the L-shaped first floor, which has the master bedroom at one end and a guest bedroom at the other. Knocking down an interior wall created an organic flow between the kitchen, living, and dining areas and allowed light to wash through from end to end. Existing sliding doors offered access and views from both the master bedroom and the dining room into the garden terrace.

OPPOSITE: A hanging swing of a window seat overlooks Central Park. A few blue accents infuse the simple, mostly neutral palette with shades of chromatic color. PAGE 96: An industrial metal cabinet repurposed as a console by the front door provides a handy place for keys. PAGE 97: Handsome and practical, indoor/outdoor matting at the entry functions beautifully in bad weather.

The client had his heart set on a sill-height window seat to enjoy the park view. Picking up on the industrial metalwork of the roof trusses, David and I designed two steel benches for the living room; hanging like swings in the dormer windows, they were positioned to make the most of the apartment's bird's-eye views. A fireplace set in a refaced wall of gray marble provided a focus for one of the room's back-to-back custom seating groups. The other was positioned to face the TV.

Inspired by the slope of the mansard roof and the canted forms of Richard Serra's tilted metal wall sculptures, we worked with metal artisan Jake DuCharme to design a curved zinc frame for the freestanding banquette—the most complicated piece I have ever done—that partially encircles the dining area. The actual fabricator of the banquette made a template for the piece, but before he constructed the seating element, he first brought the template to see if it would fit. It did not, and it took us several tries to realize why. Once we understood that the curve of the top edge had to be different than that of the base, the problem was solved. Custom dining chairs introduced yet another sensuous element to the composition.

To enlarge the kitchen, we took down a dated copper wall. The addition of a zinc bar on rusticated wooden columns blended seamlessly with the gray limestone flooring and provided an additional seating area and work surface. Voluptuous glass pendant lights from the clients' former home introduced accents of age and patina.

A palette of warm beiges and grays throughout helped to soften the effect of all the metal surfaces. A combination of rusticated, stained, and polished wood finishes and various types of polished and natural stone introduced some visual and tactile intrigue. For plushness, the luxurious, comfortable fabrics chosen for the upholstered pieces and curtains were also durable enough to stand up to the owners' much-loved pets.

OPPOSITE: The exposed roof structure prompted the interior's metal elements. PAGE 100: Back-to-back seating groups tame the volume; antique Japanese accessories add character to the shelves. PAGE 101: In this palette, nothing quite matches. PAGE 102: The rustic meets the refined. PAGE 103: My Rock vase cozies up to its real counterpart.

Richard Serra's sculptures inspired the metal-encased banquette. PAGE 106: For casual meals, a high table replaces the usual built-in. PAGE 107: A barnacle-covered vase doubles as a sculpture atop the dining area sideboard. PAGE 108: Glass mosaic walls and marble counters add to the textural conversation. PAGE 109: The counter doubles as a drainboard.

SECRETS

For any interior designer, out of sight is never out of mind. For those like me who are allergic to clutter, much of a room's power to transport depends on the spell cast by visual simplicity. But each space, no matter how sparely beautiful, also has to function seamlessly. So all of the paraphernalia—linens, dishes, vases, art supplies, toys, and so on—that correspond to the room's daily life should be close at hand. That dilemma is where the logic (and the romance) of creating another world out of view factors into each and every design scheme.

A visit to the great mansions of Newport introduced me to the idea that these kinds of hidden compartments could exist at a room-sized scale. As we toured those amazing interiors, I was so surprised to discover that what appeared to be a seamless, uninterrupted wall might in fact be a series of well-masked doors hiding perfectly fitted, luxuriously finished systems of storage. Seeing the basic components of the room's structure used as camouflage and convenience was a revelation. Understanding that I could make all the household stuff that I didn't want to look at disappear yet stay within easy reach changed my approach to design.

Hiding things in plain sight has helped me tailor each space for the people who use it. One of my clients wanted the convenience and glamour of a dressing table in her bedroom but didn't want to look at her toiletries except when she was getting ready for her day. An alcove offered just the perfect spot for the table, so we nested it there and flanked it with fitted compartments behind wooden plank walls that were actually accordion doors. Another client needed more room for her dishes and tabletop items, but the room lacked space for additional storage or furniture of any kind. Installing pullout shelving in an otherwise unused wall next to the dining room solved the problem. (Some glassware hangs at the top; plates stack at the bottom.) When she wants to set the table, she pulls out the unit and takes what she needs. The rest of the time, it disappears.

Spatial secrets can be as much about unmasking as masking. In one penthouse renovation on Central Park West, the architect and I unsheathed the building's structural support system, which had long been boxed in behind soffits. Exposing the underlying armature of steel and incorporating it into the design as a decorative item was so simple, yet so appropriate and revealing.

To uncover the mysteries of a space, or to create them, a designer must look hard, notice, and listen closely to how each client envisions living day to day. Where will this person fold the laundry? Is there a way to fashion a home office into a kind of magician's cabinet, so that it is right there in the open when up and running, but completely out of sight when it is not?

What solution satisfies a specific need without telegraphing its purpose? There are so many ways to clear the decorative decks without exposing everything. Hidden doors, disguised drawers, concealed closets, and other spatial sleights of hand come down to us from earlier, more gracious times, which is why they suit older homes so very well. Regardless of whether a space is traditional or modern, inventive spatial thinking (along with a touch of fantasy) makes for a house full of open-and-shut secrets that can do much to help us streamline the way we live.

TIME AND AGAIN

Historic houses often speak for themselves as to which decisions in a renovation will or won't make sense. This four-story Renaissance Revival townhouse in Brooklyn certainly did. As it became clear how these clients, a young family of three, wanted to inhabit their living spaces, one idea for transformation led to another and another until all the elements of the redesign fit together.

When the family purchased the house, the interiors were formal, untouchable, and decorated to the nth degree—in other words, entirely wrong for their casual, contemporary lifestyle. Every room needed a cosmetic makeover. Before the decorating, though, came several major architectural interventions, as both upstairs baths and the kitchen needed significant reinvention. In trying to be economical and convert as much of what already existed as possible, we lucked into a series of unexpected spatial relationships that allowed for surprising, functional solutions.

Typically, each floor of a townhouse like this contains a wide street-facing room and a narrower rear-facing room. Our first serious overhaul involved the kitchen and dining area. At some point in the house's life, the kitchen had migrated from the garden level (its original location) into a disproportionately small space at the rear of the second floor. With a formal dining room at the back of the parlor level one flight down, food had to be carried downstairs because there was no dumbwaiter. Then came the eureka moment: because the placement of the existing refrigerator aligned almost perfectly with a closet on the parlor level, if we moved the refrigerator and gutted the closet (outfitted as a bar), that space could serve as a shaft for a dumbwaiter. Then the leftover space

PAGE 111: Concealing a series of medicine cabinets, framed artworks—collages I created when we couldn't find pieces to fit—replace the expected mirrors. OPPOSITE: Extremely ornate woodwork such as this transforms from oppressive to handsome when allowed visual space to breathe. A pendant fixture of faceted, antiqued mirror adds glamour overhead. For a unique look, the stair carpet combines cut and loop versions of the same design.

in that wall could become pullout storage. Plus, if we borrowed space from the bathroom adjacent to the kitchen, it would free up that area for additional cabinetry and the refrigerator.

The parlor-floor living room was spacious, but very deep and narrow. Because this family loves to entertain, they wanted the ability to use the living room for both large groups and intimate gatherings. The furnishings were chosen to accomplish these goals and to make these spaces feel friendly toward contemporary life. The handful of pieces they kept from their previous home went to furnish the garden level.

The front room of the second floor became a den that doubles as an extra guest room, thanks to a queen-size mattress in the TV cabinet that slides down and rolls out with the press of a button. In the bath, formerly en suite, a newly tented shower plus added trim and moldings provide character and an out-of-the-ordinary sculptural flourish.

The master bedroom, son's bedroom—painted his favorite golden yellow—and guest room remained where they were at the top of the house. Unusually, the family preferred to share one bath. So under the existing skylight, we separated the steam shower and bathtub (for maximum efficiency and beauty), installed radiant-heat floors as in all the bathrooms, added a radiator that also serves as a towel warmer, and created a laundry cabinet that opens to a converted closet for the washer/dryer.

Framed by the surviving dark woodwork, creamy hues and spots of warm color mingle with mostly cool shades—blues, greens, turquoises— in welcoming rooms with a youthful, cheerful, sophisticated balance. For this family, the next generation, that's just what the house suggested.

OPPOSITE: The parlor's related patterns and geometries introduce complexity into an otherwise straightforward arrangement of furnishings. A live-edge coffee table adds an organic contrast. PAGE 116: A playful arrangement with elements from nature creates a whimsical still life on the console below the TV. PAGE 117: In the living room bay, a stoneware pedestal bowl by Guy Veryzer echoes the shape of the cast-resin table. One of my collages rests atop the radiator.

OPPOSITE: The pier mirror in the center of the living room is original to the house, and it is the first thing the eye sees upon entering. PAGE 120: In the dining room, light wells silhouette the intricacies of the molding and other original woodwork details. The color splash of the chair upholstery acts as an invitation. PAGE 121: A reconfigured original door fronts the newly created dumbwaiter and the two refrigerator drawers that open underneath it; on either side, concealed storage cabinets slide out of the wall as necessary. PAGE 122: The copper of the tea set echoes the orange velvet of the nearby dining chairs. PAGE 123: With a shelf hovering directly above, the radiator functions as a console table.

STILL LIFE

Sometimes a particular area of a room needs an artistic, unexpected something—or arrangement of somethings—to bring it into focus and make us look. That is where the still life enters the design process.

Each still life exists purely to please the eye, excite the imagination, and trigger the thought process. A mesmerizing effect can emerge just from the way individual textures, forms, and colors look together, without any other subtext. For that reason, variety is essential. Yet the elements needn't be expensive—they can be found objects, often organic. What matters above all is the visual relationships, the pairings of forms, textures, colors: shells filled with mosses, a dried tree fungus on a polished wood surface, an abandoned hornet's nest next to a rolled-up canvas in front of a calligraphic painting that explores every inky shade at the darker end of the spectrum. There is something in nature that is grounding, that calls to all of us. The lushness of nature's colors is impossible to duplicate by any other means.

I tend to compose each still life as I would a painting, and always for the sake of its beauty. For whatever reason, various forms may respond particularly well to one another. Compelling visual tensions can develop from the quality of the spatial relationships between components (that is, their closeness to or distance from one another). The way light travels through, glances off, or dances around each object in the grouping factors into the overall effect, as do the shadows the objects cast.

Texture, color, and pattern—and their distinct complexities—may spark an idea for an experiment in juxtapositions. Why not have the nuances of various shades of black, for example, highlighted by reflections of blue, conversing with other textures of black? Or what about an ordinary marble tray that holds a textured object next to a smooth one, paired with an intricate woven pattern and topped by a mysterious lasso-shaped piece of rusted metal found in the woods?

A still life can come together consciously or happen by accident. It almost always evolves. In our country house, a row of birds' nests atop a dining room mantel extends the mantel's reach with each new find. A charred log in the fireplace caught our eyes because of its intensely black charcoal sheen. We rescued it and placed it in front of one my husband's paintings, where for the next year we admired it as concept for an avant-garde skyscraper. The deepening relationships are what cause the intrigue, while the strangeness of the elements have their own interest. And while they are unexpected—a quality that I love—these still lifes and others are part of the property and our experience of being there.

When people have favorite objects, I love to use them. Those objects have personal meaning and attached memories that go above and beyond any intrinsic value or functional purpose. I like to leave space around them so that they can garner the proper attention they deserve, and so they can catch the light and the shadow throughout each day.

Every room needs finishing touches. Still lifes are what I envision to balance each interior, yet it is impossible to plan them out in advance. They materialize in the final stages of the design process, and they are what add the magic.

BUILDING THE DREAM

In design, there is always a behind-the-scenes story that combines the personal with the pragmatic. This is especially true when a house is new construction and intended for the future, like this two-story, four-bedroom Brooklyn residence. At the time the couple commissioned it, they were young newlyweds planning for a family to come (they now have three children). They knew they were in search of a traditional look, but not how to achieve it. I entered the picture early enough to help them reenvision what was already underway architecturally. That made it possible to create spaces that met their dreams and their needs and were imbued with the kind of design intrigue that a house such as this should have.

The addition of European details did much to recast the character of the raw spaces with a spirit of age. These details included moldings, groin vaults, pilasters, a hallway of storage paneled with hidden doors, Soane mantels for the fireplaces, and elegant materials ranging from custom-wrought ironwork to wide planks of reclaimed wood, plaster finishes, and limestone floors imported from France.

The front door opens onto a round, double-height entry hall with a domed ceiling and spiral stair. Through an arch opposite the front door, a groin-vaulted intersection marks the meeting of two passageways. One, a stairwell, descends to the basement. The other, a paneled hallway of exposed and hidden storage spaces, leads to the family room: the breakfast room, den, and kitchen combined in one, open space. To the other side of the kitchen, a smaller space houses combined formal living

PAGE 125: Wrapped and interlaced, a mass of tangled branches gathered in the woods fills an alcove with a sculpture from nature. OPPOSITE: In a circular entry hall, patterned elements—from the imported French limestone floor to the custom wrought-iron balustrade—reinforce the essential geometry. PAGE 128: From twenty-first-century avant-garde to midcentury modern to eighteenth-century-style neoclassical, the furnishings are a fresh mix of periods and styles. A Martyn Thompson fabric woven to look like a painter's drop cloth gives the armchairs a fanciful spirit. PAGE 129: A John Soane–style mantel helps to create the room's classic contemporary feeling.

and dining rooms. Throughout, the furnishings are spare, elegant, and timeless, pieces that will grow with the family and blend organically with the additions they will bring in over time. A soft palette of grays, blues, and creams reflects the couple's sensibilities and feels at one with the surrounding materials, finishes, and details. Adding to the overlay of tradition are a few key elements, including a classic eight-arm wood-and-iron chandelier over the dining table and a large gilt sconce over the living room mantel.

All the bedrooms are upstairs, under soft, graceful groin vaults that are intended to balance the slope of the roofline. The master bath, awash in natural light, features a freestanding tub placed by a window and a separate shower, as well as storage nested behind wall panels that are three invisible doors. In the children's bath, water-resistant plaster walls introduce a feeling of texture and age. All the doors and drawers open with an oversized skeleton key that, because of its size and shape, seems to be from another time.

Many of the details in these rooms are customized. Other aspects may be mass-produced, although they look anything but off the shelf in this setting. As the family evolves and the children continue to grow, no doubt these rooms will change in appearance as well. That's the magic of design.

OPPOSITE: A length of vine may not be the most obvious starting point for a floral arrangement, yet when it's placed in a vase and allowed to unfurl its tendrils naturally, it can provide a room with a living, sculptural flourish and a refreshing moment of green.

OPPOSITE: Antique Empire chairs add the perfect proportion to the room. PAGE 134: In the family room, organic forms balance stricter geometries. PAGE 135: With its flush details and the quiet contrast of blackened steel and walnut, the coffee table provides a subtle beauty. PAGE 136: The paneling conceals doors to the powder room and home office. PAGE 137: For everyday dining, benches pull up to a concrete-topped table. PAGE 138: Fewer decorative elements increase the impact of simplicity. PAGE 139: In a new home, reproduction rim-lock hardware gives a feeling of history. PAGE 140: Behind the washstand's light structure, paneled walls contain hidden doors to storage. PAGE 141: A polished-iron soaking tub invites relaxation.

OPEN SESAME

Certain projects drive home a truth that experience teaches designers time and time again: the devil is always in the details. The renovation of this 4,000-square-foot, four-bedroom Brooklyn residence fit perfectly into that category. When the clients purchased the space, it was in a state of architectural chaos. Picture four different door heights in the foyer alone, each treated individually, along with unmatched air-conditioning vents, irregular soffits, and no moldings of any kind, anywhere. My first challenge involved developing a harmonious group of details, like applied moldings, that would simplify and unify the overall appearance of the interior spaces.

The second major challenge had to do with the husband's home office, which required some out-of-the-box thinking. As an investor, he wanted a work space that would house his three computers and other necessary equipment and storage (and hide all of it when not in use) but didn't separate him from the center of his family life. For that purpose, I created a place for him in a structure within a structure between the living and dining rooms. This completely outfitted "room" opens on opposing sides like a magician's cabinet; additional storage, including filing cabinets, maximizes the use of its exterior. For a bit of decoration, the hardware combines ornamental push plates that I found years ago at a garage sale and standard cremone bolts.

To keep the space as calm and light as possible, the couple asked for a neutral color palette, which I love. They also requested furnishings that

OPPOSITE: This renovation focused on finessing the interior architecture through moldings and other decorative details to establish a harmonious environment. That effort also included the creation of a huge cabinet between the living and dining rooms. The space behind the closed doors converts from a home office to serving space, and additional storage was built into its exterior surround. Variations on the entry's brilliant yellow walls (SEE PAGE 146) bring a golden glow to the living room's otherwise neutral palette.

their youngest child and dog couldn't damage, so there is nothing fragile in the mix of contemporary and traditional designs. For durability and ease of maintenance, outdoor fabrics cover all the upholstered pieces. The living room rug features a pattern that should hide any canine wear and tear. And since every quiet palette needs at least a spot of boldness for contrast, we plastered the foyer walls in a brilliant, glowing shade of yellow.

Their modern kitchen, while functional, also needed its details addressed, especially the task lighting, which was irregular and spotty. Replacing (and hiding) fixtures under cabinets solved that problem while also providing additional illumination. Tweaking a few other details—like incorporating vents in the moldings—rendered the surfaces much cleaner and less cluttered with unattractive wires and outlets.

The master bedroom had its own set of spatial difficulties, among them an asymmetrical window that threw off the placement of the bed. To disguise that irregularity and create the illusion of symmetry, we stretched a curtain from corner to corner behind the bed. An antique stone mantel helped add character to the space, and we also commissioned a large painting to lend its texture to the mix and provide a backdrop for the dressing table.

The two older children had very specific ideas about their bedrooms, and each was involved in the selection of the preferred color palette, furnishings, and decorative objects. For the nursery, the animal portraits set the tone. What could be more charming?

OPPOSITE: At the back of the built-in shelving, a linen lining hides the speakers of the A/V system. The linen press stows additional office equipment, including the printer. PAGE 146: Composite leaf ornamentation over a handblown, iridescent glass panel contrasts with the fluted crown molding. PAGE 147: The other side of the cabinet faces the dining area.

OPPOSITE: When working at home, the client wanted to be in the thick of family life; the computer screens move easily when necessary. PAGE 150: In the master bedroom, a curtain behind the bed resolves an awkwardly placed window and soffit. For intensity of color, nothing outdoes velvet. PAGE 151: The antique mantel adds rich texture to the palette. PAGES 152–153: For textural interest, a large, abstract painting acts as a backdrop for her dressing table and antique mirror. PAGES 154–155: The mix of old and new styles continues in the daughter's room. PAGE 156: A menagerie is adorable company in a nursery. PAGE 157: There's no need to abandon elegance and sophistication in a baby's room.

HOME AGAIN

Most of us feel a deep sentimental attachment to our homes, especially those where we raised our children. This couple certainly did. Although they have several homes around the country, they've kept this house, their longtime family seat in the suburbs, because all three generations love to gather here to spend summertime together.

When the two of them came to me, they knew they wanted to upgrade their living spaces while keeping many of the furnishings they love. More than that, they wanted to finally fix the house's architectural issues, which included dark rooms, poor sight lines, and more. Replacing all the windows and doors proved completely transformational, as did introducing unifying details and repeating materials throughout for consistency.

Our first move was to open up the foyer to the dining room and the expansive view of nature beyond. Then we scaled and replaced the stair, adding elegance with stone borders, softness underfoot with an inset carpet, and a flush molding with a narrow reveal for interest and minimalist simplicity. That singular flourish inspired us to fold a similar reveal into all the main spaces. The dining room got a slate floor to mimic an existing inset medallion in the foyer, and the living room floor was upgraded with wider planks.

Refreshing the dining room involved some sleight of hand to enhance functionality and beauty. The couple liked the shape of their existing buffet and the storage it provided, so we kept it but reinvented it with a different wood finish, doors covered in hammered copper, custom hardware hammered with the same patina, and drawers and shelves newly lined with felt.

In the living room, we also retained many of their existing pieces, recovering here, recoloring there, making the most of design's cosmetic options.

OPPOSITE: With only a slit in the wall to give a glimpse of the rooms beyond, the original entry felt closed and dark. Opening the space up to the rest of the interior and focusing the sight lines on a full floor-to-ceiling view of the back garden through the dining room transformed the entire experience of the house. The gong is the client's own.

A holdover from years ago, the circular yellow rug had long occupied the room's center. To establish a different kind of symmetry, we pushed it up against the hearth, cutting off one section to make it look as if the missing portion were tucked underneath the wall. Repositioning the existing light fixture helped change the room's balance, as did relocating the table, now with a new leather top, and custom-designed chairs into the rug's field. At the space's opposite end, we arranged a separate TV area for quiet viewing; nestled into a convenient niche, a custom cabinet (shaped like a secretary with horsehair doors) houses the TV and doubles as a bar.

The kitchen also received a complete overhaul. It originally opened to the den via a pass-through window. Since the wife had always felt isolated from activities when she was cooking, we joined the two into one space. The introduction of a floor-to-ceiling window opened the view to the backyard and the trees beyond and helped flood the kitchen area with light; silvered-brass plates installed behind new custom cabinets enhanced the effect. The couple felt strongly about keeping their breakfast table and chairs, so we created a pull-up counter, rather like a sushi bar, at the proper chair height.

The den had always been lined with open shelves housed in dark wood cabinets. We decided to paint the cases white, reconfigure the interiors for better storage, and add doors to hide all the necessities. Cutting down the breakfast table to fit between the cabinets provided the wife with the accessible desk she'd never had. The pantry lives inside the den between the kitchen and fireplace, secreted in a remarkable custom armoire with a commanding visual presence. Recessing a TV over a rebuilt fireplace simplified that wall. Most of the furniture was theirs, which we re-covered. The few additions? A small table and comfortable chairs for when the room is theirs alone for an intimate evening for two.

OPPOSITE: A major aspect of the renovation involved simplifying the existing interior architecture to create visual coherence. Completely rebuilding the staircase with stone borders around the carpet runner and adding the understated detail of the reveal gave the passageway to the upstairs a quiet elegance.

OPPOSITE: Custom hammered-copper drawer fronts pick up tones from the floor. PAGE 164: By the fireplace, a chair of my design pulls up to the card table. PAGE 165: A wall-to-wall sofa expands available seating in a narrow space. PAGE 166: Horsehair-covered doors and a sterling-silver key pull add interest. PAGE 167: The living room cabinet was designed to house a bar and a built-in TV. PAGE 168: The kitchen cabinets' silvered-brass backing reflects light beautifully. PAGE 169: Installing a sushi-style counter allowed for the reuse of existing chairs. PAGES 170 AND 171: In a space shared by the kitchen and den, an original armoire designed to resemble the kitchen cabinets provides an elegant, practical solution for pantry storage. PAGE 172: Trimmed to fit, a former breakfast table now serves as a desk. PAGE 173: Restructuring the fireplace mantel allowed the flat-screen TV to sit almost flush to the wall.

REINVENTION

Interior design has a remarkable capacity to pull us into a world that is different from—and more beautiful than—the one on the other side of our front door. I started to appreciate this fantasy aspect of home as a child, thanks to one of my grandmothers. Walking into her house was like stepping into an earlier century. Her rooms were full of Americana that she had nursed and cajoled back to functionality—broken antiques and damaged vintage pieces that she had collected here, there, and everywhere and either restored or turned into something else. She used these old things daily, whether they matched or not. Her garage was always an interesting obstacle course of salvaged items awaiting her imagination and care. The idea of reinvention was central to her world and to her life at home, as it is to mine.

As the proverb goes, "Waste not, want not." Envisioning ways to reimagine favorite pieces of furniture within a new scheme stretches our powers of invention. A solution might be as straightforward as cutting down a much-loved dining table to fit into the smaller space of a breakfast area. Or it might be as off the beaten path as inserting hand-hammered copper panels into the front doors of a dark wood server to enliven its appearance and introduce some much-needed patina into a very modern room. That the patina might also pick up on the colors of the slate floor is an extra benefit!

While remade and reinvented items tend to have a practical side, they don't necessarily have to show that side of themselves first—or at all. Installing an old horse's trough in a walkway of our country house, for example, brought character to a space by introducing a sense of age and original function to a newly constructed house that resembles an old carriage house. That trough has turned out to be a great place for rinsing vegetables straight from the garden before bringing them into the kitchen. Plus, it can double as the perfect cooler for drinks during a summer party.

A certain spirit of adventure also goes along with reimagining how the practical elements of the exterior might work and look. A compost pile in a country yard doesn't have to be a row of three bins purchased from the garden store. Ours, which I turn every so often, lives inside a piece of land art that we snaked across our property. We started with a group of logs we found piled high around the trunk of a tree at the edge of the forest. As we were hauling them—they were suffocating that tree—we started to arrange them into a winding earthwork. Now whenever a tree on the property falls, we cut it up and add the pieces to the pile.

Design gives us more than one way to think about a set of circumstances, especially when the elements of fantasy and imagination come into play. With a contemporary or minimalist approach, a space can take on a meditative quality. With traditional furnishings and fabrics, it may cast a spell that speaks to other times and places. Which do we prefer? That is a matter of personal choice. But the power of interior design to reinvent furnishings, objects, and entire worlds—that's what inspires my creativity.

THE WORK OF ART

When collectors of contemporary art commission interiors for a home, the designer faces an interesting task because the rooms need to let the art speak. Spaces such as these become silent partners to the daily experience of living and looking—there but not there, beautiful but not competitive. Should the architecture of the house be a rigorous work of art itself, as this minimalist Hudson Valley, New York, retreat by the Swiss firm of HHF Architects + Ai Weiwei is, the challenge of creating appropriate decoration grows in complexity because the results must ultimately be so restrained.

The clients had a very sophisticated aesthetic and preferred a minimalist environment to provide a beautiful contrast to the surrounding bucolic landscape. They asked for contemporary, simple pieces with no heavy textures and a refined rather than rustic selection of materials. Color was kept to a minimum, with a calm, quiet palette—mostly whites and neutrals—because of the art.

Because the house was designed to show the art, the focus of the rooms was inward, notwithstanding the carefully calculated and spectacularly framed views. From my perspective, that meant the shapes and the materials of the furnishings mattered above all else. Every piece selected had a distinctive character, but its sculptural quality and its simplicity of

PAGE 175: A request to transform a favorite possession so that it fits into an evolving interior may lead to interesting, beautiful results. This server, for example, took on a different character when individually hammered-copper door panels replaced its old yellow drawer fronts. OPPOSITE: Within strong, minimalist architecture, a wall-mounted sculptural console table by Zaha Hadid and a cloud chandelier provide a subtle drama.

form took precedence. And since there was nothing competing with the art for visual attention, the sparseness of the living environment became a source of serenity.

The front door opened to an enormous foyer, where a hanging console table by Zaha Hadid gave a taste of what was to come. In the double-height living room, occasional seating and overscaled upholstery pieces were grouped to take prime advantage of the interior and exterior vistas. Steps away—and separated by a fireplace—was the dining room. Again, we kept to simple, elemental, geometric forms: a sleek plank of a table with upholstered benches of blackened steel. Against a far wall, an Ai Weiwei sculpture, one of many Chinese pieces in the clients' collection, made its presence felt. A minimalist kitchen with a small table and chairs was next to the living room, and a guest bedroom occupied the far reaches of this floor. As in the rest of the interior, elemental forms took precedence here along with textural polish.

Upstairs, a balcony with the couple's home office overlooked the living and dining areas. All warm wood tones and sculptural midcentury forms, it continued the refined organic language established below. This floor also housed a guest bedroom and the master suite, which included a bath divided by a two-sided fireplace. With such spare, disciplined rooms, the art did speak. So did nature. The overall effect was one of quiet, peace, and contemplation—everything a country house should be.

OPPOSITE: Rooms kept consciously spare with minimal furnishings allow the clients' collection of contemporary Chinese art and the house's carefully choreographed views to have maximum visual impact. PAGES 180–181: The living area's color palette complements the tonal subtleties of a painting from Cai Guo-Qiang's Gunpowder series that dominates the wall over the sofa. PAGES 182-183: With suede-upholstered blackened-steel benches, the furniture in the dining area adheres to the aesthetic. A whimsical Ai Weiwei sculpture of double tables climbs the wall.

OPPOSITE: A café table and two contemporary wing chairs create an intimate dining area in the kitchen. PAGES 186–187: A felt carpet and midcentury furnishings provide an atmosphere of productive calm in the home office; Zhan Wang's chrome scholar's rock introduces a reflective contrast to the earthy finishes. PAGES 188–189: In the master bedroom, restrained furnishings and surfaces allow the view to dominate. PAGE 190: An artisanal felt blanket in the guest bedroom offers a stark yet understated response to the smooth surfaces. PAGE 191: The master bath is a seamless structure in Corian.

ESCAPE TO NATURE

Sometime around 2002, I read an article in the *Wall Street Journal* about Wyndcliffe Mansion, a ruin of a place in Rhinebeck, New York, that some people say may have been the source of the phrase "keeping up with the Joneses." The house had been built in 1853 by Elizabeth Schermerhorn Jones, a member of the Astor family and Edith Wharton's aunt, on a site with the most spectacular views of the Hudson River Valley. The story fascinated me, as did the history of the region and the idea of the crumbling pile of a house, so my husband and I decided to go take a look. Predictably, we were inspired. When my husband suggested a year or two later that we look for land in that area to build a Chinese garden, I thought, Well, why not just find a property with a house? My closest friend introduced us to this one, which we purchased in 2004.

At the time we moved in, we knew the house had many good qualities in addition to its charm. In particular, it seemed to have a sense of peacefulness amid the wilderness. There was relief, also, in the fact that the house wouldn't need much work because it was comparatively new. Even so, the property still felt like a construction site, with piles of logs needing removal from the front yard and not a single landscape feature except for the swimming pool. One lone tree at the clearing's edge was so swallowed by an enormous pile of logs that we worried it would die.

PAGES 192–193: Tall grasses form a corridor for the stairs to the house. OPPOSITE: Set amid a carpet of stones brought from the woods, our Chinese tea table, which was carved from a single block of stone, overlooks the Hudson Valley. PAGES 196–197: Snaking through the property, our ever-changing log sculpture conceals the compost pile. PAGE 198: We stack our fireplace logs in a convenient, covered area just outside the house. PAGE 199: On hot days, the roofed exterior living room offers welcome shade. The coffee table is an architectural fragment; the Mexican mask has been in my life since childhood.

My husband and I used those logs to make a sinuous sculpture—like a fence, but not—that now hides the compost. The rest of the place was wild, which we loved. But we also wanted to have certain planned and planted spaces around the house for contrast. It took years of working outside to develop, plant, and trim the garden and the spaces we use as outdoor rooms for relaxing and dining.

The original owner had built the house in 2002 as a weekend residence, and he seems to have modeled the structure after a turn-of-the-twentieth-century carriage house. He put three bedrooms and two baths on the second floor under the eaves, where a hayloft and a caretaker's living quarters would have been. The first floor he gave over to the public areas, including a living room, small dining room, kitchen, and powder room. The finished basement has a concrete floor, which offered my husband the perfect place to paint.

I wanted a challenge for the interiors, so I pushed myself to create a different kind of look than is my tendency. Most of the wall colors we left as we found them, but we gradually switched out certain details—light fixtures, hardware, and curtains—and hung our own artwork to add depth and character. The dining room walls, for example, have always been a deep shade of blue; that is not a color I would have selected, but the effect is embracing. The addition of plain linen panels at the window brought the room more into our aesthetic realm, as did the furnishings, a

OPPOSITE: Architectural fragments add formal detail to the lap pool. PAGE 202: The Japanese print belonged to my grandparents. PAGE 203: More interesting without its case, an antique wall clock reveals its inner workings. PAGES 204–205: In the living room, two of Wenda's calligraphy paintings flank a desk purchased in China. PAGE 206: An abandoned wasp nest has its own beauty of structure, texture, and color. PAGE 207: Our rooms reflect our lives immersed in art and design. PAGES 208–209: The upholstered pieces are prototypes of my own designs. The antique child's rocker is from nearby Hudson.

mixture of Chinese pieces, vintage purchases from nearby dealers, family heirlooms, and several of my own furniture design prototypes (living room sofas, a chest of drawers, a canopy bed), as well as my husband's art pieces (a chair and desk with inset video monitors from his *United Nations* series). Every time the thought occurs to change the shade of the dining room walls or the woodwork finish, I opt not to—the deep colors create a Victorian flavor that feels so right for the idea of the house.

The master bedroom's yellow walls and floral linen print were preexisting as well. That fabric! Although its busy pattern is not one I would ever choose, I decided to remove it from a headboard that was left behind and reuse it on my canopy bed design. I also kept the window treatments, turning the fabric back to face the front to tone down the effect. What remained was a faded version of the original, which felt quite appealing. The desk chair was also a reinvention with intent. When we found it in an antique shop in nearby Hudson, it was covered in muslin and had a little stain on the seat. As a quick cleanup and to give it a unique personality, I painted over the seat with the wall paint, leaving the creases in the exposed muslin to frame the surfaces with light borders.

About a year after we moved in, my husband made one of his regular trips to China. While he was there, he had purchased all sorts of furniture for this house—antiques, reproductions, large, small, stone, wood, and so on—everything from baskets, stone tea tables, desks, and benches to

OPPOSITE: Ancient terra-cotta Chinese tomb slabs top the coffee table. PAGE 212: Turkey feathers from the yard bring nature indoors. PAGE 213: A Pierre Chareau piano stool contrasts perfectly with the 1785 pianoforte. PAGES 214–215: The dining room table—two put together to make a square—was part of Wenda's mystery purchase from China. PAGE 216: Prototypes of my porcelain designs mingle with other tableware. PAGE 217: Hand-painted bowls come from the Beijing flea market. PAGE 218: Changing the paint color and hardware brought an existing kitchen into our aesthetic. PAGE 219: The kitchen's vintage style is inspired by old carriage house cabinetry. PAGE 220: A beautifully textured Portuguese olive oil jug punctuates a corner. PAGE 221: Quirky spaces, such as this built-in window seat with storage, are what attracted us to the house.

inscribed terra-cotta panels that once lined a tomb in China. When he got back to the States, he didn't remember anything—not one detail of what would be arriving! Until his acquisitions turned up, all we could do was hope that whatever they turned out to be, they would work in the spaces. Once they did, the first challenge was finding a place for each piece. The second was moving the heavier pieces, like the massive stone table that is the centerpiece of our outdoor dining area, into position once we'd decided where they were to go. The delivery driver had dumped them out of the back of the truck onto the driveway, and that's where they stayed until we could figure out how to move them. A few weeks later, my closest friend and her brother were visiting. He suggested we try a forklift. It proved useless. At that point, we resorted to the ancient Egyptian method for transporting stones for the pyramids: pushing each one inch by inch by inch. Eventually, my husband and our friend managed to move that table all the way around the corner of the house and into place. To get the other table, a three-foot square cut from one block of stone, to its post on the opposite side of the house, they had to repeat the same slow, laborious process. Then they had to do it again with the stools, which are also heavy, though they're tiny by comparison. Suffice it to say, those tables aren't going anywhere, ever. As for the Chinese garden, even with all that we have done here over the years, it is the one feature that we originally envisioned for the property but never built.

OPPOSITE: Mixing elements of East and West, I designed our rosewood bed to incorporate the room's existing fabric. PAGES 224–225: Remaking the curtains inside out calmed the pattern's effect. PAGE 226: An upholstery tack border adds a subtle detail. PAGE 227: We chose the industrial ladder for its sculptural quality. PAGES 228–229: A headboard painted on the wall shifts focus to the copy of an Abbott Henderson Thayer work I made as an art student. PAGE 230: The tripod table and 1950s swivel chairs are Hudson finds. PAGE 231: My daughter's dollhouse started as a weekend project; designing in miniature totally captivated me. PAGES 232–233: My great uncle brought the larger dolls back from Shanghai; the others we discovered in Hudson. PAGE 235: The architectural remnant that is our outdoor coffee table demonstrates the richness of patina.

TIME

Time touches us all, in design and in life. But the question of whether or not to expose history, to show the age and past lives of the objects and furnishings we surround ourselves with—that's a personal choice. Mine is obvious. I love the textures that time creates, whether it's the lines of laughter in a face, threadbare areas that dapple a vintage silk velvet, or scars of repair in an old pewter dish or antique hope chest. The crazing on a salvaged porcelain sink. The worn paint on an old Windsor chair. These traces of longtime use are part of the unique beauty of many functional items, especially those that in their way have somehow also become art.

Suppose an interior has been home to one or more families over the decades or centuries. Instead of renovating it into a state of shiny, fresh perfection, it can be so interesting to strip away the layers of its past lives yet leave remnants of paint finishes, wallcoverings, plaster details, and stenciling for all to see. Think of it like this: Does it make sense to restore the Roman forum to its ancient pristine status? Or Pompeii to an imagined original state of glory? Why do that? When so much history remains, it makes sense—and art—to simplify the surroundings so the surviving traces of time become the focus.

I love the austerity of a simple room. But it must be balanced with something very rich to focus the eye and draw attention. When a sparely decorated room contains an antique piece, it is impossible not to cross the threshold, luxuriate in the space, and admire the beauty of that special piece up close—the luster of the wood, the detailing of the metal, the way it feels to the touch of the hand. Less really is more. When that one object is the main attraction, it becomes possible to appreciate it in full. It's like going into an antiques shop that's stuffed from wall to wall with furniture and being unable to see or appreciate one item among the crowd because of the visual overload. But take any one of those pieces and put it in a room all by itself. Suddenly, it—and the room—come to life. The surprise is that both are even more beautiful than imagined.

Antiques introduce a patina to interiors when they are contemporary and sparse. Folding family heirlooms and children's artwork into our rooms helps to create a continuum of life and personal meaning. When we bring art, objects, and furnishings into our homes, we bring their stories, too. Even if their value is purely sentimental, they help us define where we came from, and, perhaps, how we became who we are.

RESOURCES

ANTIQUES

1stdibs
1stdibs.com
vintage furnishings, objects,
lighting

Arenskjold Antiques Art
www.arenskjold.com
(518) 828-2800
vintage furnishings, lighting,
objects

Boiseries et Décorations
www.boiseries-deco.fr
+33 01 43 71 76 30
doors, windows, architectural
antiques

Chateau Domingue
www.chateaudomingue.com
(713) 961-3444
architectural antiques, antique
lighting, decorative surfaces

City Foundry
www.cityfoundry.com
(718) 923-1786
vintage furnishings, objects

Cottage Treasures
www.cottagetreasuresonline.com
(908) 876-1580
vintage furnishings, lighting,
architectural antiques, objects

Dienst + Dotter Antikviteter
www.dienstanddotter.com
(212) 861-1200
Scandinavian antiques, lighting,
objects

Evergreen Antiques
www.evergreenantiques.com
(212) 744-5664
Scandinavian antiques

Found Objects of Industry
www.foundobjectsofindustry.com
(610) 944-1711
architectural antiques, lighting,
hardware, objects

Holler & Squall
www.hollerandsquall.com
(347) 223-4685
vintage furnishings, objects

Hostler Burrows
www.hostlerburrows.com
(212) 343-0471
vintage furnishings, objects,
lighting

Lost City Arts
www.lostcityarts.com
(212) 375-0500
vintage furnishings, lighting,
objects

Red Chair on Warren
www.redchair-antiques.com
(518) 828 1158
antique furnishings, linens,
tableware

Rural Residence
www.ruralresidence.com
(518) 822-9259
decorative objects

Shibui
www.shibui.com
(718) 875-1119
Japanese antiques and objects

Urban Archaeology
www.urbanarchaeology.com
(212) 431-4646
architectural antiques,
reproduction lighting, plumbing,
hardware, decorative surfaces

Vincent Mulford Antiques
(518) 828-5489
antique furnishings, lighting,
objects

ART AND OBJECTS

Cheryl Hazan Gallery
www.cherylhazan.com
(212) 343-8964
contemporary art

De Vera
www.deveraobjects.com
(212) 625-0838
quirky objects

J. Lohmann Gallery
www.jlohmanngallery.com
(212) 734-1445
decorative objects

Robin Rice Gallery
www.robinricegallery.com
(212) 366-6660
photographs

WendaGu'Studio
www.wendagu.com
(718) 935-0425
+86 130 0316 6951
contemporary art

DECORATIVE MATERIALS

Bark House
www.barkhouse.com
(828) 765-9010
bark wall surfaces

Lithea
www.lithea.it
+39 0941050123
stone surfaces, objects, sinks

Stone Farm
www.stonefarmliving.com
(877) 977-0004
reclaimed stone

FABRICS

Amy Pilkington
www.amypilkington.com
tie-dyed fabrics

Penn & Fletcher
www.pennandfletcher.com
(718) 361-9498
embroidery

Talini
www.talinihome.com
(434) 989-9801
bed and table linens

FANS

Woolen Mill Fan Company
www.architecturalfans.com
(717) 382-4754
reproduction vintage fans

FIREPLACES

Chesneys
www.chesneys.com
(646) 840-0609
mantels

FLOORING

Delbasso
www.delbasso.it
+39 0828 307383
wood flooring materials

Paris Ceramics
www.parisceramicsusa.com
(888) 845-3487
decorative stone, tile, wood

FURNISHINGS

Alexander Lamont
Angela Brown
(212) 627-5757

Andrianna Shamaris
www.andriannashamarisinc.com
(212) 388-9898
organic furnishings, architectural
antiques

Caleb Woodard Furniture
www.calebwoodardfurniture.com
(615) 380-8595
unique furnishings

Charles H. Beckley
www.chbeckley.com
(212) 759-8450
custom mattresses

Chun Zai
www.chunzaitaipei.com
+886 02 2708 8689
contemporary Chinese furnishings

Edward Ferrell + Louis Mittman
www.ef-lm.com
(336) 841-3028
upholstered furnishings

KGBL Furniture
www.kgblnyc.com
(212) 420-7866
modern furnishings

Matter
www.mattermatters.com
(212) 343-2600
contemporary furnishings, lighting,
objects

Matthias Pliessnig
www.matthias-studio.com
unique furnishings

Muse Designs
Alison Legge
ELAN ATELIER
415.326.8200
www.elanatelier.com
bronze lighting, furnishings,
objects

Ot/tra
www.ot-tra.com
(718) 682-3045
unique wood furnishings

Roman Thomas
www.romanthomas.com
(212) 473-6774
classic furnishings

Sawaya & Moroni
+39 02 863951
unique furnishings

Skram
www.skramfurniture.com
(336) 222-6622
fine furnishings

Studio Van den Akker
www.studiovandenakker.com
(212) 644-3535
unique and mid-century style
furnishings

Tara Shaw
www.tarashawmaison.com
(504) 525-1131
classic furnishings, objects,
antiques

Uhuru Design
www.uhurudesign.com
(718) 855-6519
unique furnishings

WP Sullivan
www.wpsullivan.com
(718) 784-8480
unique furnishings, lighting

GLASS

Michael Davis Glass
www.michaeldavisglass.com
(718) 383-3712
blown glass

Miriam Ellner
www.miriamellner.com
(212) 807-6316
verre églomisé

Thomas Fuchs Creative
https://tfcreative.myshopify.com
(917) 549-1281
hand-blown glasses, lamps,
objects

HARDWARE

Dauby
www.dauby.be/en/
+32 3 354 1686
specialized hardware

P.E. Guerin
www.peguerin.com
(212) 243-5270
specialized hardware

Van Cronenburg
www.petervancronenburg.be
(646) 745-0404
architectural hardware, lighting

Whitechapel
www.whitechapel-ltd.com
(800) 468-5534
reproduction hardware

KITCHENS AND APPLIANCES

Abimis Kitchens
www.abimis.com
+39 0422 8021
kitchen cabinets

Stealth Kitchen Modules
www.yestertec.com
(610) 443-0172
hidden compact kitchens

The Vintage Fridge Company
www.thevintagefridgecompany.
com
+44 07813 293 866
rebuilt iceboxes

LIGHTING AND ELECTRICAL DEVICES

David Wiseman Studio
www.dwiseman.com
(323) 834-2672
artisanal lighting, objects

The Electric Candle Company
www.electric-candle.com
(866) 753-6966
candle flame bulbs

Forbes & Lomax
www.forbesandlomax.com
(212) 486-9700
light switches

Sandra Liotus Lighting Design
www.sandraliotuslightingdesign.
com
(401) 845-9236
art lighting

Trufig
www.trufig.com
(800) 582-7777
electrical devices

The Urban Electric Co.
www.urbanelectricco.com
(843) 723-8140
decorative lighting

METALWORK

Amuneal
www.amuneal.com
(800) 755-9843
custom metalwork

La Forge de Style
www.laforgedestyle.com
(201) 488-1955
custom ironwork

Metalmorfis
(413) 237-3441
custom metalwork

MILLWORK

American Woods & Veneers
www.americanwoodsinc.com
(718) 937-2195
custom millwork, kitchens,
furniture

Risa Meyer
www.risameyer.com
+47 41 16 13 32
Risa staircase

PLASTER AND PAINT

Architectural Sculpture and
Restoration
www.asrnyc.com
(516) 535-1224
plaster moldings

Calcem
www.limepaint.com
(305) 576-9070
lime paint

Domingue Architectural Finishes
www.dominguefinishes.com
(713) 961-5270
lime plaster, lime paint

Ionic Casting
(718) 786-7670
plaster moldings

Surface & Architecture Workshop
www.saaw.com
(215) 636-0677
decorative surfaces

Stephen Antonson
www.stephenantonson.com
Dessin Fournir Showroom
(215) 758-0844
plaster lighting, furniture, mirrors,
objects

PLUMBING

Antonio Lupi
www.antoniolupi.it
(305) 432-3933
minimalist bath fixtures

CEA
www.ceadesign.it
+39 0424 572309
minimalist bath and kitchen
fixtures

LooLoo Design
www.looloodesign.com
(800) 508-0022
vintage plumbing

Metropolitan Home Hardware
and Bath
(718) 801-8550
bath and kitchen fixtures,
hardware and lighting

Pibamarmi
www.pibamarmidesign.com
+39 0444 688775
minimalist bath fixtures

TABLEWARE AND ACCESSORIES

Artel
www.artelglass.com
+420 226 254 700
glassware

davistudio
www.davistudio.com
(518) 392-7308
porcelain dinnerware

KSDS Porcelain
www.ksdsporcelain.com
(718) 935-0425
porcelain accessories

Saikai
www.saikaiusa.com
(310) 322-4500
tabletop, kitchenware,
accessories

UPHOLSTERY AND WINDOW TREATMENTS

Doreen Interiors
(212) 255-9008
upholstery, window treatments

JGeiger
www.jgeigershading.com
(844) 543-4437
roller shades

Sandringham
(212) 594-9210
upholstery, window treatments

ACKNOWLEDGMENTS

My deepest appreciation goes to my husband, Wenda Gu, whose great talent helped me fine-tune my own ability to see. You have been my constant inspiration for years.

I am grateful to have begun my career at Vignelli Associates in New York. The design sense of Lella and Massimo Vignelli has become the foundation of my vision today. I will never forget either of you.

Thank you to all my clients, who trusted me with the single most important places in their lives: the homes where their family memories are made. It has been a great pleasure to collaborate with you over the years.

Thank you to the talented authors who included my work in their books. To Ingrid Abramovitch for Restoring a House in the City, Carl Dellatore for Interior Design Master Class, Barbara Sallick for The Perfect Bath, and Andrea Mingfai Chu for Modern Shanghai Vintage Houses and Shanghai Interiors. I feel honored to be a part of your work.

To all the editors, both domestic and foreign, who supported me by publishing my interiors. I feel so fortunate to have received your attention. Special appreciation to Metropolitan Home, as my first publication; it inspired me to have con-fidence in myself. Thank you to Wang Xu of AD China, whose support always made me feel appreciated as a local.

To everyone at Rizzoli and especially my editor, Kathleen Jayes, for your continual support and enthusiasm. I couldn't be more thrilled to be a part of the Rizzoli family.

This could never have happened without the vision and ability of Jill Cohen, who knew exactly how to assemble all the perfect components to create a book from a mere dream.

Thanks to Doug Turshen and David Huang, who amazingly curated endless photos into a sequence that beautifully describes my story, while guiding me through the possibilities.

To William Abranowicz, who has effortlessly captured the essence of my vision. I thoroughly enjoyed the process of reimagining the most familiar spaces in my daily life from a fresh viewpoint. My heartfelt thanks to all the talented pho-tographers who have shot my work for various publications over the years. A special thanks for the contributions seen here to Ellen McDermott, who has created beautiful photos for me for years, and Nikolas Koenig.

To Judith Nasatir, who magically found words to create my story when I couldn't imagine how to begin. You made this long task seem easy.

Thanks to the architects David Foley of Foley Fiore Architecture and HHF Architects + Ai Weiwei, whose beautiful work is seen within. I am honored to have collaborated with you.

I am forever grateful to the contractors and their suppliers who made my vision a reality through their endless atten-tion to detail. Your work makes my work look better. To DPD Builders, Design Build Enterprises, MJM Contracting, Gotham Contractors, ZZZ Carpentry, and Carey Contracting. I am especially grateful to Marty Berger of Homart Homes, who more than thirty years ago allowed me to join his construction team. I can't imagine a better design school than that experience; it transformed my understanding of architecture and design.

Thank you to the multitude of vendors and artisans who have worked closely with us over the years so that we pro-vide the best product we can. We appreciate your collaboration, endless samples, attention to details, and loans to help clients envision how small things can make big differences in their homes. Special gratitude to my husband, Wenda Gu, for always having extraordinary artwork for me to try in clients' homes; to Dane Owen at Shibui for work-ing with us to find the perfect accents to enliven a room; to Dena Zemsky for her amazing ceramics; to the team at Studio Van den Akker for their complete willingness to provide what I need at the very moment I need it; to those at Edward Ferrelll + Louis Mittman, who laboriously adjust custom pieces until they fit and look perfect; to Martin Grub-man at P.E. Guerin, who lets me spend hours sorting through the archive bins to find perfectly shaped hardware (so much fun!), then makes it work; to Louis Rodriguez at Patterson Flynn Martin, who always finds the right carpet no matter how challenging; to Richard Peng, founder of American Woods & Veneers, whose precision has resulted in flawless custom cabinetry regardless of the difficulties; to Leonard Schechter from Found Objects of Industry (and originally Urban Archaeology), who has always made architectural antiques function properly in their new settings; and to the many others who have become endeared to me due to their hard work and dependability. We are all noth-ing in this industry without each other's help.

I would not be where I am today without the years of dedication of Lisa Marchisotto, who was instrumental to all fac-ets of my office. To Anthony Pellino and Wendy Zhang, who created years of beautiful detailed work and drawings, ensuring results that make all of us proud. To LMA Consultants, who have helped me manage the business of design so I can continue to do the work I enjoy.

To my family members, each of whom played a part that led me to the path I took, which has given me a fulfilling life. What more can one hope for?

OPPOSITE: In a house with restrained, classically inspired details, a custom bronze-and-glass railing brings in a contemporary touch.
PAGE 241: In our Brooklyn living room, the light creates mystery as it travels across the different textures.

First published in the United States of America in 2018
by Rizzoli International Publications, Inc.
300 Park Avenue South
New York, NY 10010
www.rizzoliusa.com

© 2018 Kathryn Scott

All rights reserved. No part of this publication may be reproduced,
stored in a retrieval system, or transmitted in any form or by any means,
electronic, mechanical, photocopying, recording, or otherwise,
without prior consent of the publishers.

Designed by Doug Turshen with David Huang

All images by William Abranowicz except the following:
Page 177, 182/183,185,186/187,188/189, 190, 191 by Ellen McDermott
Page 179,180/181 by Nikolas Koenig

2018 2019 2020 2021 / 10 9 8 7 6 5 4 3 2 1

Distributed in the U.S. trade by Random House, New York

Printed in China

ISBN-13: 978-0-8478-6178-1

Library of Congress Catalog Control Number: 2017957097